D0502603

*Practicing Peace*
*in Times of War*

*Books by Pema Chödrön*

Comfortable with Uncertainty
No Time to Lose
The Places That Scare You
Practicing Peace in Times of War
Start Where You Are
When Things Fall Apart
The Wisdom of No Escape

# Practicing Peace
# in Times of War

## PEMA CHÖDRÖN

BASED ON TALKS EDITED BY
Sandy Boucher

SHAMBHALA
Boston & London
2006

SHAMBHALA PUBLICATIONS, INC.
Horticultural Hall
300 Massachusetts Avenue
Boston, Massachusetts 02115
www.shambhala.com

9 8 7 6 5 4 3 2 1

First Edition
*Printed in the United States of America*

⊚ This edition is printed on acid-free paper that meets
the American National Standards Institute z39.48 Standard.
Distributed in the United States by Random House, Inc.,
and in Canada by Random House of Canada Ltd

*Designed by Lora Zorian*

LIBRARY OF CONGRESS CATALOGING-IN-PUBLICATION DATA
Chödrön, Pema.
Practicing peace in times of war/
Pema Chödrön; based on talks edited by
Sandy Boucher.—1st ed.
p.   cm.
ISBN-13: 978-1-59030-401-3 (alk. paper)
ISBN-10: 1-59030-401-2
1. Peace—Religious aspects—Buddhism. 2. Religious life—
Buddhism. 3. Buddhism—Doctrines.
I. Boucher, Sandy. II. Title.
BQ4570.P4.C56 2006
294.3'37273—dc22
2006013417

If somebody doesn't begin to provide some kind of harmony, we will not be able to develop sanity in this world at all.

Somebody has to plant the seed so that sanity can happen on this earth.

—CHÖGYAM TRUNGPA RINPOCHE

# Contents

# Acknowledgments

THE WRITINGS in this book are inspired by my teachers Chögyam Trungpa Rinpoche and Dzigar Kongtrul Rinpoche. In particular I want to thank Kongtrul Rinpoche for the teachings on *shenpa* that I discuss in chapter 3.

I would like to thank my editors, Sandy Boucher and Eden Steinberg, as well as Hilda Ryūmon Gutiérrez Baldoquín, who typed the changes to the manuscript and offered many valuable suggestions. Thanks also to Emily Hilburn Sell for first editing my talk on *shenpa,* which is the basis for chapter 3. I also gratefully acknowledge my friend Acharya Dale Asrael for the term "compassionate abiding," which I use in chapter 5.

My appreciation goes also to Gigi Sims, who transcribed the talks, and again to Eden Steinberg, who conceived of this book and patiently guided it to completion.

*Practicing Peace*
*in Times of War*

## I

# *Practicing Peace in Times of War*

WAR AND PEACE start in the hearts of individuals. Strangely enough, even though all beings would like to live in peace, our method for obtaining peace over the generations seems not to be very effective: we seek peace and happiness by going to war. This can occur at the level of our domestic situation, in our relationships with those close to us. Maybe we come home from work and we're tired and we just want some peace; but at home all hell is breaking loose for one reason or another, and so we start yelling at people. What is our motivation? We want some happiness and ease and peace, but what we do is get even more worked up and we get everyone else worked up too. This is a familiar scenario in our homes, in our workplaces, in our communities, even when we're just driving our cars. We're just driving along and someone cuts in front of us and then what? Well, we don't like it, so we roll down the window and scream at them.

War begins when we harden our hearts, and we harden them easily—in minor ways and then in quite serious, major ways, such as hatred and prejudice—whenever we feel uncomfortable. It's so sad, really, because our motivation in hardening our hearts is to find some kind of ease, some kind of freedom from the distress that we're feeling.

Someone once gave me a poem with a line in it that offers a good definition of peace: "Softening what is rigid in our hearts." We can talk about ending war and we can march for ending war, we can do everything in our power, but war is never going to end as long as our hearts are hardened against each other.

What happens is a chain reaction, and I'd be surprised if you didn't know what I'm talking about. Something occurs—it can be as small as a mosquito buzzing—and you tighten. If it's more than a mosquito—or maybe a mosquito is en-ough for you—something starts to shut down in you, and the next thing you know, imperceptibly the chain reaction of misery begins: we begin to fan the grievance with our thoughts. These thoughts become the fuel that ignites war. War could be that you smash that little teensy-weensy mosquito. But I'm also talking about war within the family, war at the office, war on the streets, and also war between nations, war in the world.

We often complain about other people's fundamentalism. But whenever we harden our hearts, what is going on with us? There's an uneasiness and then a tightening, a shutting down, and then the next thing we know, the chain reaction begins and we become very righteous about our right to kill the mosquito or yell at the person in the car or whatever it might be. We ourselves become fundamentalists, which is to say we become very self-righteous about our personal point of view.

Jarvis Masters, who is a prisoner on

death row, has written one of my favorite spiritual books, called *Finding Freedom*. In a chapter called "Angry Faces," Jarvis has his TV on in his cell but he doesn't have the sound on because he's using the light of the TV to read. And every once in a while, he looks up at the screen, then yells to people down the cell block to ask what's happening.

The first time, someone yells back, "It's the Ku Klux Klan, Jarvis, and they're all yelling and complaining about how it's the blacks and the Jews who are responsible for all these problems." About half an hour later, he yells again, "Hey, what's happening now?" And a voice calls back, "That's the Greenpeace folks. They're demonstrating about the fact that the rivers are being polluted and the trees are being cut down and the animals are being hurt and our

Earth is being destroyed." Some time later, he calls out again, "Now what's going on?" And someone says, "Oh, Jarvis, that's the U.S. Senate and that guy who's up there now talking, he's blaming the other guys, the other side, the other political party, for all the financial difficulty this country's in."

Jarvis starts laughing and he calls down, "I've learned something here tonight. Sometimes they're wearing Klan outfits, sometimes they're wearing Greenpeace outfits, sometimes they're wearing suits and ties, but they all have the same angry faces."

I remember reading once about a peace march. When one group was coming back from the march, some pro-war people started cutting them off and blocking them; everyone started screaming and hitting each other. I thought, "Wait a minute, is there something wrong with this picture? Clobbering people with your peace sign?" The next time you get angry, check out your righteous indignation, check out your fundamentalism that supports your hatred of this person, because this one really is bad—this politician, that leader, those heads of big companies. Or maybe it's rage at an individual who has harmed you personally or harmed your loved ones. A fundamentalist mind is a mind that has become rigid. First the heart closes, then the mind becomes hardened into a view, then you can justify your hatred of another human being because of what they represent and what they say and do.

If you look back at history or you look at any place in the world where religious groups or ethnic groups or racial groups or political groups are killing each other, or families have been feuding for years and years, you can see—because you're not particularly invested in that particular argument—that there will never be peace until somebody softens what is rigid in their heart. So it's necessary to take a big perspective on your own righteousness and your own fundamentalism when it begins to kick in and you think your own aggression and prejudice are reasonable.

I try to practice what I preach; I'm not always that good at it but I really do try. The other night, I was getting hard-hearted, closed-minded, and fundamentalist about somebody else, and I remembered this expression that you can never hate somebody if you stand in their shoes. I was angry at him because he was holding such a rigid view. In that instant I was able to put myself in his shoes and I realized, "I'm just as riled up, and self-righteous and closed-minded about this as he is. We're in exactly the same place!" And I saw that the more I held on to my view, the more polarized we would become, and the more we'd be just mirror images of one another—two people with closed minds and hard hearts who both think they're right, screaming at each other. It changed for me when I saw it from his side, and I was able to see my own aggression and ridiculousness.

If you could have a bird's-eye perspective on the Earth and could look down at all the conflicts that are happening, all you'd see are two sides of a story where both sides think they're right. So the solutions have to come from a change of heart, from softening what is rigid in our hearts and minds.

One of the most inspiring modern examples we have of this is the civil rights movement. I was recently rereading the writings of Martin Luther King Jr., and I understood once again that the whole movement was based on love—love that doesn't exclude anybody. This is also the Buddhist idea of love. In this view, you want everybody to be healed.

Now, some political activists might say, "OK, but nothing will ever change just by holding that all-inclusive, loving view." But the truth is, when you take that view and you begin to live by it, at the level of your own heart in your own everyday life, something begins to shift very dramatically, and you begin to see things in a different way. You begin to have the clarity to see injustice happening, but you can also see that injustice, by its very definition, is harming everybody involved. It's harming the people who are being oppressed or abused, and it's harming those who are oppressing and abusing.

And from a Buddhist point of view, those who are being oppressed have a chance—just as people did in the civil rights movement—to be purified by what is happening to them. They have the opportunity to let hatred be replaced by love and compassion and to try to bring about change by nonviolence and nonaggression. Instead of sinking into self-absorption they have a chance to let their suffering link them with the suffering of all beings—those harming, those helping, and those feeling neutral. In other words, they have a chance to soften what is rigid in their hearts and still hold the view that injustice is being done and work toward unwinding that injustice or that cruelty.

But those who are oppressing may be

so prejudiced and rigid in their minds that there's very little opportunity for them to grow and learn. So they're the ones who ultimately suffer the most, because their own hatred and anger and prejudice continue to grow. There is nothing that causes more pain and suffering than to be consumed by bigotry, to be consumed by cruelty and anger.

So war and peace start in the human heart. Whether that heart is open or whether that heart closes has global implications.

Recently, I was teaching from a Buddhist text called *The Way of the Bodhisattva*, which offers guidance to those who wish to dedicate their lives to alleviating suffering and to bringing benefit to all sentient beings. This was composed in the eighth century in India by a Buddhist master named

Shantideva. In it he has an interesting point to make about peace. He says something along the lines of, "If these long-lived, ancient, aggressive patterns of mine that are the wellspring only of unceasing woe, that lead to my own suffering as well as the suffering of others, if these patterns still find their lodging safe within my heart, how can joy and peace in this world ever be found?"

Shantideva is saying that as long as we justify our own hard-heartedness and our own self-righteousness, joy and peace will always elude us. We point our fingers at the wrongdoers, but we ourselves are mirror images; everyone is outraged at everyone else's wrongness.

And then Shantideva makes another thought-provoking point. He says that the people who we get so upset at, they eventually move away or they die. And likewise, with nations that fight each other, time passes and either the nations no longer exist or they shift alliances and enemies become allies. He reminds us how everything changes with time. But the negative seeds that are left in our mindstream, the impact of our hatred and our prejudice, is very long-lived. Why so? Because as long as we keep strengthening our anger and self-righteousness with our thoughts and our words and our actions, they will never go away. Instead, we become expert at perfecting our habits of hard-heartedness, our own particular brand of rigid heart and closed mind.

So what I'm advocating here is something that requires courage—the courage to have a change of heart. The reason this requires courage is because when we don't do the habitual thing, hardening our heart and holding tightly to certain views, then we're left with the underlying uneasiness that we were trying to get away from. Whenever there's a sense of threat, we harden. And so if we don't harden, what happens? We're left with that uneasiness, that feeling of threat. That's when the real journey of courage begins. This is the real work of the peacemaker, to find the soft spot and the tenderness in that very uneasy place and stay with it. If we can stay with the soft spot and stay with the tender heart, then we are cultivating the seeds of peace.

I think to do this kind of work it's very helpful to take some kind of personal vow. You make it clear in your own mind what you wish for and then you make a vow. For instance, let's say you hit your children and it's habitual, but then you make a vow to yourself: "Whatever happens, I'm not going to hit them." You seek help and you look everywhere for ways to help you not hit them when that uneasiness arises and everything in you wants to close your heart and mind and go on automatic pilot and do the thing that you always hate yourself for doing. You vow that to the best of your ability—knowing that sometimes there's going to be backsliding, but nevertheless, to the best of your ability—you vow not to cause harm to yourself or to anybody else, and to actually help yourself and your children.

This kind of vow should be put in words that are meaningful and true to you so they aren't somebody else's good thoughts but actually your own highest, heartfelt wish for yourself. Your motivation behind the vow is that you equate it with the ultimate kindness for yourself, not the ultimate punishment or the ultimate shaping up, like "I'm bad, I need to shape up."

No, the basic view is that there's nothing wrong with you or me or anybody else.

It's like what the Zen Master Suzuki Roshi once said. He looked out at his students and said, "All of you are perfect just as you are *and* you could use a little improvement." That's how it is. You don't start from the view of "I'm fundamentally messed up and I'm bad and therefore I have to get myself into shape." Rather the basic situation is good, it's sound and healthy and noble, *and* there's work that we need to do because we have ancient habits, which we've been strengthening for a long time and it's going to take a while to unwind them.

Living by a vow is very helpful, and actually it's Jarvis Masters who caused me to think about this. His Tibetan teacher, Chagdud Tulku Rinpoche, went to San Quentin Prison and, through the glass, talking through a telephone, did an empowerment ceremony in which Jarvis took the vow to never cause harm and to the best of his ability to try to help. He has lived by these vows so earnestly, and when I read his book sometimes I laugh out loud at the extremes to which he has to go not to cause harm in a place like San Quentin.

To prevent some hostile, disrespectful guards from being killed, for instance, he had to talk some angry inmates into flooding their cells because they needed a way to express their rage. He knew that if he didn't come up with something, they were planning to retaliate by stabbing the guards. So instead he said, "Listen, the whole thing is, you don't need to kill them. These guys are wanting to get out of here to go to a party so you just need to ruin their day by making them work late cleaning up the mess we'll make." And everyone bought it, so they just flooded the tier.

One of my favorite stories about Jarvis was when he unintentionally helped some other inmates connect with the absolute, vast quality of their own minds. There is a teaching that says that behind all hardening and tightening and rigidity of the heart, there's always fear. But if you touch fear, behind fear there is a soft spot. And if you touch that soft spot, you find the vast blue sky. You find that which is ineffable, ungraspable, and unbiased, that which can support and awaken us at any time. And somehow Jarvis, in this story of trying to avert harm, conveyed this fundamental openness to the other inmates.

One day there was a seagull out on the yard in San Quentin. It had been raining and the seagull was there paddling around in a puddle. One of the inmates picked up something in the yard and was about to throw it at the bird. Jarvis didn't even think about it—he automatically put out his hand to stop the man. Of course this escalated the man's aggression and he started yelling. Who the hell did Jarvis think he was? And why did Jarvis care so much about some blankety-blank bird?

Everyone started circling around, just waiting for the fight. The other inmate was screaming at Jarvis, "Why'd you do that?" And out of Jarvis's mouth came the words, "I did that because that bird's got my wings."

Everyone got it. It simply stopped their minds, softened their hearts, and then there was silence. Then they all started laughing and joking with him. Even years later, they still tease him, "What did you mean, Jarvis,

'That bird's got my wings'?" But at that moment, everyone understood.

If we begin to take responsibility for our own self-righteousness, it leads to empathy. Here's one more Jarvis story to illustrate this. Many of the prison guards in San Quentin are very kind and helpful, but some of them get mean and unreasonable and take their frustrations out on the prisoners. That day there had been plenty of that happening and tempers were short. An inmate came up to Jarvis in the yard and asked, "Is it your Buddhism that keeps you so calm, Jarvis? How can you stand it when these guards are giving you such shit?"

And Jarvis said, "Oh, it has nothing to do with Buddhism. I just think that if I retaliate, they'll go home and beat their kids. I don't want that to happen to any of those little kids." The other man got it completely. Our empathy and wisdom begin to come forward when we're not clouded by our rigid views or our closed heart. It's common sense. "If I retaliate, then they'll go home and beat their kids, and I don't want that happening."

There are many stories, but the basic message I'm trying to convey is that to the degree that each of us is dedicated to wanting there to be peace in the world, then we have to take responsibility when our own hearts and minds harden and close. We have to be brave enough to soften what is rigid, to find the soft spot and stay with it. We have to have that kind of courage and take that kind of responsibility. That's true spiritual warriorship. That's the true practice of peace.

# 2

# *The Courage to Wait*

I F THE JUSTIFIED aggression of men and women just like us is the cause of war, then how do we ordinary folks go about finding peace? When we feel aggression in any of its many forms—resentment, discrimination, jealousy, complaining, and so forth—it's hard to know what to do. We can apply all the good advice we've heard and given to other people. But often all that doesn't seem to help us.

Traditionally, it's taught that patience is the antidote to aggression. When I heard this the first time, it immediately caught my interest. I thought, if patience is really the antidote to aggression, maybe I'll just give it a wholehearted try. In the process I learned about what patience is and about what it isn't. I would like to share with you what I've understood and to encourage you to find out for yourself how patience can dissolve the mean-heartedness that results in us harming one another.

Most importantly, I learned about patience and the cessation of suffering—I learned how patience is a way to de-escalate aggression and its accompanying pain. This is to say that when we're feeling aggressive—and I think this would go for any strong emotion—there's a seductive quality that pulls us in the direction of wanting to get some resolution. We feel restless, agitated, ill at ease. It hurts so much to feel the aggression that we want it to be resolved. Right then we could change the way we look at this discomfort and practice patience. But what do we usually do? We do exactly what is going to escalate the aggression and the suffering. We strike out, we hit back. Someone insults us and, initially, there is some softness there—if you can practice patience, you can catch it—but usually you don't even realize there was any softness. You find yourself in the middle of a hot, noisy, pulsating, wanting-to-get-even state of mind. It has a very unforgiving quality to it. With your words or your actions, in order to escape the pain of aggression, you create more aggression and pain.

I recently read a letter from a U.S. soldier in Iraq. He wrote about the so-called enemy fighters, the unknown people who are so filled with pain and hate that they sit in the dark waiting to kill foreign soldiers like him. When they succeed, and his friends' bodies are blown into unrecognizable pieces, he just wants revenge. He said that each day he and his fellow U.S. soldiers were also becoming men who wait in the darkness hoping to kill another human being. As he put it, "We think that by striking back we'll release our anger and feel better, but it isn't working. Our pain gets stronger day by day." Amid the chaos and horror of war, this soldier has discovered a profound truth: if we want suffering to lessen, the first step is learning that keeping the cycle of aggression going doesn't help. It doesn't bring the relief we seek, and it doesn't bring happiness to anyone else either. We may not be able to change the outer circumstances, but we can always shift our perspective and dissolve the hatred in our minds.

So when you're like a keg of dynamite just about to go off, patience means just slowing down at that point—just pausing—instead of immediately acting on your usual, habitual response. You refrain from acting, you stop talking to yourself, and then you connect with the soft spot. But at the same time you are completely and totally honest with yourself about what you are feeling. You're not suppressing anything; patience has nothing to do with suppression. In fact, it has everything to do with a gentle, honest relationship with yourself. If you wait and don't fuel the rage with your thoughts, you can be very hon-est about the fact that you long for revenge; nevertheless you keep interrupting the torturous story line and stay with the underlying vulnerability. That frustration, that uneasiness and vulnerability, is nothing solid. And yet it is painful to experience. Still, just wait and be patient with your anguish and with the discomfort of it. This means relaxing with that restless, hot energy—knowing that it's the only way to find peace for ourselves or the world.

Patience has a quality of honesty and it also has the quality of holding our seat. We don't automatically react, even though inside we *are* reacting. We let all the words go and are just there with the rawness of our experience.

Fearlessness is another ingredient of patience. If you want to practice patience that leads to the cessation of suffering, to the de-escalation of aggression, it means cultivating a fearlessness that is both compassionate and brave. Because at this point you're getting to know anger and how it easily breeds violent words and actions, and this can be decidedly unnerving. You can see where your anger will lead before you do anything. You're not repressing it, you're just sitting there with the pulsating energy—going cold turkey with the aggression—and you get to know the naked energy of anger and the pain it can cause if you react. You've followed the tug so many times, you already know. It feels like an undertow, that desire to say something mean, to seek revenge or slander, that desire to complain, to just somehow spill out that aggression. But you slowly realize that those actions don't get rid of aggression, they increase it. Instead you're patient—patient with yourself—and this requires the gentleness and courage of fearlessness.

———

Developing patience and fearlessness means learning to sit still with the edginess of the discomforting energy. It's like sitting on a wild horse, or maybe even more like a wild tiger that could eat you up. There is a limerick to that effect: "There was a young lady of Niger who smiled as she rode on a tiger. They came back from the ride with the lady inside, and the smile on the face of the tiger." Sitting with our uneasiness feels like riding on that tiger.

When we stick with this process we learn something very interesting: there is no resolution for these uncomfortable feelings. This resolution that human beings seek comes from a tremendous misunderstanding: we think that everything can become predictable and secure. There is a basic ignorance about the truth of impermanence, the truth of the fleeting groundless nature of all things. When we feel powerful energy, we tend to be extremely uncomfortable until things are fixed in some kind of secure and comforting way, either on the side of "yes" or the side of "no," the side of "right" or the side of "wrong." We long for something that we can hold on to.

But the practice of patience gives us nothing to hold on to. Actually, the Buddhist teachings, in general, give us nothing to hold on to. In working with patience and fearlessness, we learn to be patient with the fact that not only us but everyone who is born and dies, all of us as a species, are naturally going to want some kind of resolution to this edgy, moody energy. And there isn't any. The only resolution is temporary and ultimately just causes more suffering. We discover that joy and happiness, a sense of inner peace, a sense of harmony and of being at home with yourself and your world come from sitting still with the moodiness of the energy until it rises, dwells, and passes away. It never resolves itself into something solid. We stay in the middle. The path of touching in on the inherent softness of the genuine heart is sitting still, being patient with that kind of unformed energy. And we don't have to criticize ourselves when we fail, even for a moment, because we're just completely typical human beings; the only thing that's unique about us is that we're brave enough to go into these things more deeply and explore beneath our surface reaction of trying to get solid ground under our feet.

Patience is an enormously supportive and even magical practice. It's a way of completely shifting the fundamental human habit of trying to resolve things by either going to the right or the left, labeling things "good" or labeling them "bad." It's the way to develop fearlessness, the way to contact the seeds of war and the seeds of lasting peace—and to decide which ones we want to nurture.

Patience and curiosity also go together. You wonder, "Who am I?" Who am I at the level of my neurotic patterns? Who am I beyond birth and death? If you wish to look into the nature of your own being, you need to be inquisitive. This path is a journey of self-reflection, beginning to look more closely at what's going on in our mind and heart. The meditation practices give us suggestions on how to look, and patience is an essential component for this looking. Aggression, on the other hand, prevents us from seeing clearly; it puts a tight lid on our curiosity. Aggression is an energy that is determined to resolve the situation into some kind of solid, fixed, very hard pattern where somebody wins and somebody loses. There is no room for open-ended curiosity or wonder.

If you have already embarked on this journey of self-reflection, you may be at a place that everyone, sooner or later, experiences on the spiritual path. After a while it seems like almost every moment of your life you're there, where you realize you have a choice. You have a choice whether to open or close, whether to hold on or to let go, whether to harden or soften, whether to hold your seat or strike out. That choice is presented to you again and again and again.

Perhaps each one of us has made the discovery that behind resistance—definitely behind aggression and jealousy—behind any kind of tension, there is always a soft spot that we're trying to protect. Someone's actions hurt our feelings and before we even notice what we're doing, we armor ourselves in a very old and familiar way. So we can either let go of our solid story line and connect with that soft spot or we can continue to stubbornly hold on, which means that the suffering will continue.

But it requires patience even to be curious enough to look, to self-reflect. And when you realize you have a choice to stay still or to act out it requires great patience to stick with that edgy feeling and not escalate the suffering. You almost automatically speed up or shut down, you involuntarily seek solid ground, and you'll frequently feel afraid. You may feel that if you let go and simply feel the energy you're going to die, or something is going to die. And you're right. If you let go, something will die, but it's something that will benefit you greatly.

I've come to find that patience also has humor and playfulness. It's a misunderstanding to think of it as endurance, as in "just grin and bear it." Endurance involves some kind of repression or trying to live up to somebody else's standards of perfection. Instead, you find that it helps to be able to laugh at what you see as your own imperfections. Patience could be a synonym for gentleness and loving-kindness. You can develop patience and loving-kindness and a sense of humor for your own imperfections, for your own limitations, for not living up to your own high ideals. Someone once came up with a slogan, which is, "Lower your standards and relax as it is." That's a slogan for patience.

---

In Tibetan Buddhism there's a set of teachings for cultivating compassion called mind training, or *lojong*. One of the *lojong* teachings is, "Whichever of the two occurs, be patient." This means if a painful situation occurs, be patient, and if a pleasant situation occurs, be patient. This is an interesting point. Usually, we jump all the time; whether it's pain or pleasure, we want resolution. So if we're happy and something is great, we could also be patient then, and not fill up the space, going a million miles an hour—impulse shopping, impulse talking, impulse acting out.

I'd like to stress yet again that the thing we have to be most patient with is when we find ourselves being despondent about our inability to do any of this. For patience to lead to the cessation of suffering, for it to develop into fearlessness and genuine curiosity, we need to be patient with our-selves just as we are.

There's another *lojong* teaching that says, "One in the beginning and one at the end"; when you wake up in the morning you can begin your day with an aspiration, for instance, you might say, "I'm going to try today to the best of my ability to prac-tice patience." And then at the end of your day you look back over all you did with lov-ing-kindness and you're patient with the fact that when you review the last eight hours, or even review the last twenty min-utes, you discover, "I was impatient and ag-gressive in the same style that I've been as long as I can remember; I got carried away with irritation exactly the same way I al-ways do."

Then the path of peace depends on being patient with the fact that all of us make mistakes. And that's more important than getting it right. This whole process seems to work only if you're willing to give yourself a break, to soften up, as you practice patience. As with the rest of the teachings, you can't win and you can't lose. You don't get to just say, "Well, since I never can do it, I'm not going to try." It's like you never can do it and still you try. And, interestingly enough, that adds up to something, it adds up to appreciation for yourself and for others. It adds up to there being more warmth in the world. You look out through your eyes and you just see yourself wherever you go—you see all these people who are escalating their suffering just like you do. You also notice people catching themselves just like you do, and they give you the gift of their fearlessness. You begin to be grateful for even the slightest gesture of bravery on the part of others because you know it's not so easy. Their courage increases your trust in the basic goodness of yourself and all beings throughout the world—each of us just wanting to be happy, each of us not wanting to suffer.

# 3

# *Not Biting the Hook*

I<small>N</small> T<small>IBETAN</small> there is a word that points to the root cause of aggression, the root cause also of craving. It points to a familiar experience that is at the root of all conflict, all cruelty, oppression, and greed. This word is *shenpa*. The usual translation is "attachment," but this doesn't adequately express the full meaning. I think of *shenpa* as "getting hooked." Another definition, used by Dzigar Kongtrul Rinpoche, is the "charge"—the charge behind our thoughts and words and actions, the charge behind "like" and "don't like." Here's an everyday example: Someone criticizes you. She criticizes your work or your appearance or your child. In moments like that, what is it you feel? It has a familiar taste, a familiar smell. Once you begin to notice it, you feel like this experience has been happening forever. That sticky feeling is *shenpa*. And it comes along with a very seductive urge to do something. Somebody says a harsh word and immediately you can feel a shift. There's a tightening that rapidly spirals into mentally blaming this person, or wanting revenge or blaming yourself. Then you speak or act. The charge behind the tightening, behind the urge, behind the story line or action is *shenpa*.

You can actually feel *shenpa* happening. It's a sensation that you can easily recognize. Even a spot on your new sweater can take you there. Someone looks at us in a certain way, or we hear a certain song, or walk into a certain room and boom. We're hooked. It's a quality of experience that's not easy to describe but that everyone knows well.

Now, if you catch *shenpa* early enough, it's very workable. You can acknowledge that it's happening and abide with the experience of being triggered, the experience of urge, the experience of wanting to move. It's like experiencing the yearning to scratch an itch, and generally we find it irresistible. Nevertheless, we can practice patience with that fidgety feeling and hold our seat.

In these moments, we can contact the

underlying insecurity of the human experience, the insecurity that is inherent in a changing, shifting world. As long as we are habituated to needing something to hold on to, we will always feel this background rumble of slight unease or restlessness. We want some relief from the unease, so when *shenpa* arises we go on automatic pilot: without a pause, we follow the urge and get swept away.

Mostly we don't catch *shenpa* at an early stage. We don't catch the tightening until we've already indulged the urge to scratch our itch in some habitual way. In fact, unless we equate not acting out with friendliness toward ourselves, this refraining can feel like putting on a straitjacket and we struggle against it.

The best way to develop our ability to stay fully present with *shenpa* and to equate that with loving-kindness is in meditation. This is where we can train in not getting swept away.

Meditation teaches us how to open and relax with whatever arises, without picking and choosing. It teaches us to experience the uneasiness and the urge fully and to interrupt the momentum that usually follows. We do this by not following after the thoughts and learning to return again and again to the present moment. We train in sitting still with the itch of *shenpa* and with our craving to scratch. We label our story lines "thinking" and let them dissolve, and we come back to "right now," even when "right now" doesn't feel so great. This is how we learn patience, and how we learn to interrupt the chain reaction of habitual responses that otherwise will rule our lives.

You can also begin to notice *shenpa* in

other people. You're having a conversation with a friend. At one moment her face is open and she's listening, and the next you see her eyes glaze over or her jaw tense. What you're seeing is her *shenpa,* and she may not be aware of it at all. When peace is your goal, this is an important observation.

From your side, you can keep going in the conversation, but now with a kind of innate intelligence and wisdom called *prajna*. This is clear seeing of what's happening.

Without being blinded by your own story line or trying to get some ground under your feet, you simply recognize your friend's *shenpa* and you practice patience— you give the situation some space. You have the innate intelligence to realize that when you're discussing something that needs to happen in the office, or trying to make a point with one of your children, or your partner, that nothing is going to get through right now because this person has just been hooked.

So simply by recognizing what's happening we can nip aggression or craving in the bud—our own and that of others. As we become more familiar with doing this, our wisdom becomes a stronger force than *shenpa*. That in itself has the power to stop the chain reaction. One method of doing this is to bring your awareness to your breath, strengthening your ability to be there openly and with curiosity. You might also change your way of talking at that point and ask, "How do you feel about what I just said?" The other person might say, curtly, "It's fine, no problem." But you know enough to be patient and maybe nonaggressively say something like "Let's talk about this again later," understanding that even simple words like this can avert two people from going to war.

Our training is to acknowledge when we're tensing, when we're hooked, when we are all worked up. The earlier we catch it, the easier *shenpa* is to work with; but nevertheless, if we catch it even when we're all worked up, that's good enough.

Sometimes we even have to go through the whole cycle and end up making a mess. The urge is so strong, the hook is so sharp, the habit is so entrenched, that there are times we can't do anything about it.

But what you can always do is this: after the fact, you can self-reflect and rerun the story. Maybe you start with remembering the all-worked-up feeling and get in touch with that. You can reexperience the *shenpa* very vividly and experiment with not getting carried away. This is very helpful.

We could think of this process in terms of the four Rs: *recognizing* the *shenpa, refraining* from scratching, *relaxing* with the underlying urge to scratch, and then *resolving* to interrupt the momentum like this for the rest of our lives. What happens when you don't follow the habitual response? You're left with the underlying energy. Gradually you learn to relax into that shaky, impermanent moment. Then you resolve to do your best to keep practicing this way.

I once saw a cartoon of three fish swimming around a hook. One fish is saying to the others, "The secret is nonattachment." That's a *shenpa* joke: the secret is don't bite that hook. If we can learn to relax in the place where the urge is strong, we will get a bigger perspective on what's happening. We might come to see that there are two billion kinds of itch and seven quadrillion types of scratching, but we just call the whole thing *shenpa*.

# 4

# *Changing Our Attitude Toward Pain*

O N  A  V E R Y  B A S I C level all beings think that they should be happy. When life becomes difficult or painful, we feel that something has gone wrong. This wouldn't be a big problem except for the fact that when we feel something's gone wrong, we're willing to do anything to feel okay again. Even start a fight.

According to the Buddhist teachings, difficulty is inevitable in human life. For one thing, we cannot escape the reality of death. But there are also the realities of aging, of illness, of not getting what we want, and of getting what we don't want. These kinds of difficulties are facts of life. Even if you were the Buddha himself, if you were a fully enlightened person, you would experience death, illness, aging, and sorrow at losing what you love. All of these things would happen to you. If you got burned or cut, it would hurt.

But the Buddhist teachings also say that this is not really what causes us misery in our lives. What causes misery is always trying to get away from the facts of life, always trying to avoid pain and seek happiness—this sense of ours that there could be lasting security and happiness available to us if we could only do the right thing.

In this very lifetime we can do ourselves and this planet a great favor and turn this very old way of thinking upside down. As Shantideva points out, suffering has a great deal to teach us. If we use the opportunity when it arises, suffering will motivate us to look for answers. Many people, including myself, came to the spiritual path because of deep unhappiness. Suffering can also teach us empathy for others who are in the same boat. Furthermore, suffering can humble us. Even the most arrogant among us can be softened by the loss of someone dear.

Yet it is so basic in us to feel that things should go well for us, and that if we start to feel depressed, lonely, or inadequate, there's been some kind of mistake or we've lost it. In reality, when you feel depressed, lonely, betrayed, or any unwanted feelings, this is an important moment on the spiritual path. This is where real transformation can take place.

As long as we're caught up in always looking for certainty and happiness, rather than honoring the taste and smell and quality of exactly what is happening, as long as we're always running away from discomfort, we're going to be caught in a cycle of unhappiness and disappointment, and we will feel weaker and weaker. This way of seeing helps us to develop inner strength. And what's especially encouraging is the view that inner strength is available to us at just the moment when we think we've hit the bottom, when things are at their worst.

Instead of asking ourselves, "How can I

find security and happiness?" we could ask ourselves, "Can I touch the center of my pain? Can I sit with suffering, both yours and mine, without trying to make it go away? Can I stay present to the ache of loss or disgrace—disappointment in all its many forms—and let it open me?" This is the trick.

There are various ways to view what happens when we feel threatened. In times of distress—of rage, of frustration, of failure—we can look at how we get hooked and how *shenpa* escalates. It can also be helpful to shift our focus and look at how we put up barriers. In these moments we can observe how we withdraw and become self-absorbed. We become dry, sour, afraid; we crumble, or harden out of fear that more pain is coming. In some old familiar way, we automatically erect a protective shield and our self-centeredness intensifies. But this is the very same moment when we could do something different. Right on the spot, through practice, we can get very familiar with the barriers that we put up around our hearts and around our whole being. We can become intimate with just how we hide out, doze off, freeze up. And that intimacy, coming to know these barriers so well, is what begins to dismantle them. Amazingly, when we give them our full attention they start to fall apart.

Ultimately all the practices I have mentioned before are simply ways we can go about dissolving these barriers. Whether it's learning to be present through sitting meditation, acknowledging *shenpa,* or practicing patience, these are methods for dissolving the protective walls that we automatically put up.

---

When we're putting up the barriers and the sense of "me" as separate from "you" gets stronger, right there in the midst of difficulty and pain, the whole thing could turn around simply by *not erecting barriers;* simply by staying open to the difficulty, to the feelings that you're going through; simply by not talking to ourselves about what's happening. That is a revolutionary step. Becoming intimate with pain is the key to changing at the core of our being—staying open to everything we experience, letting the sharpness of difficult times pierce us to the heart, letting these times open us, humble us, and make us wiser and more brave. Let difficulty transform you. And it will. In my experience, we just need help in learning how not to run away.

If we're ready to try staying present with our pain, one of the greatest supports we could ever find is to cultivate the warmth and simplicity of *bodhichitta*. The word *bodhichitta* has many translations, but probably the most common one is "awakened heart." The word refers to a longing to wake up from ignorance and delusion in order to help others do the same. Putting our personal awakening in a larger—even planetary framework—makes a significant difference. It gives us a vaster perspective on why we would do this often difficult work. There are two kinds of *bodhichitta:* relative and absolute. Relative *bodhichitta* includes compassion and *maitri*. Chögyam Trungpa Rinpoche translated *maitri* as "unconditional friendliness with oneself." This unconditional friendliness means having an unbiased relationship with all the parts of your being. So, in the context of working with pain, this means making an intimate, compassionate, heart-relationship with all those parts of ourselves we generally don't want to touch.

Some people find the teachings I offer helpful because I encourage them to be kind to themselves—but this does not mean pampering our neurosis. The kindness that I learned from my teachers, and that I wish so much to convey to other people, is kindness toward all qualities of our being. The qualities that are the toughest to be kind to are the painful parts, where we feel ashamed, as if we don't belong, as if we've just blown it, when things are falling apart for us. *Maitri* means sticking with ourselves when we don't have anything, when we feel like a loser. And it becomes the basis for extending the same unconditional friendliness to others.

If there are whole parts of yourself that

you are always running from, that you even feel justified in running from, then you're going to run from anything that brings you into contact with your feelings of insecurity. And have you noticed how often these parts of ourselves get touched? The closer you get to a situation or a person, the more these feelings arise. Often when you're in a relationship it starts off great, but when it gets intimate and begins to bring out your neurosis, you just want to get out of there. So I'm here to tell you that the path to peace is right there, when you want to get away.

You can cruise through life not letting anything touch you, but if you really want to live fully, if you want to enter into life, enter into genuine relationships with other people, with animals, with the world situation, you're definitely going to have the experience of feeling provoked, of getting hooked, of *shenpa*. You're not just going to feel bliss. The message is that when those feelings emerge, this is *not* a failure. This is the chance to cultivate *maitri,* unconditional friendliness toward your perfect and imperfect self.

Relative *bodhichitta* also includes awakening compassion. One of the meanings of *compassion* is "suffering with," being willing to suffer with other people. This means that to the degree you can work with the wholeness of your being—your prejudices, your feelings of failure, your self-pity, your depression, your rage, your addictions— the more you will connect with other people out of that wholeness. And it will be a relationship between equals. You'll be able to feel the pain of other people as your own pain. And you'll be able to feel your own pain and know that it's shared by millions.

Absolute *bodhichitta,* also known as *shunyata,* is the open dimension of our being, the completely wide-open heart and mind. Without labels of "you" and "me," "enemy" and "friend," absolute *bodhichitta* is always here. Cultivating absolute *bodhichitta* means having a relationship with the world that is nonconceptual, that is unprejudiced, having a direct, unedited relationship with reality.

That's the value of sitting meditation practice. You train in coming back to the unadorned present moment again and again. Whatever thoughts arise in your mind, you regard them with equanimity and you learn to let them dissolve. There is no rejection of the thoughts and emotions that come up; rather, we begin to realize that thoughts and emotions are not as solid as we always take them to be.

It takes bravery to train in unconditional friendliness, it takes bravery to train in "suffering with," it takes bravery to stay with pain when it arises, and not run or erect barriers. It takes bravery to not bite the hook and get swept away. But as we do, the absolute *bodhichitta* realization, the experience of how open and unfettered our minds really are, begins to dawn on us. As a result of becoming more comfortable with the ups and the downs of our ordinary human life, this realization grows stronger.

We start with taking a close look at our predictable tendency to get hooked, to separate ourselves, to withdraw into ourselves, and put up walls. As we become intimate with these tendencies, they gradually become more transparent and we see that there's actually space, there is unlimited, accommodating space. This does not mean that then you live in lasting happiness and comfort. That spaciousness includes pain. We may still get betrayed, may still be hated. We may still feel confused and sad. What we won't do is bite the hook. Pleasant happens. Unpleasant happens. Neutral happens. What we gradually learn is to not move away from being fully present.

We need to train at this very basic level because of the widespread suffering in the world. If we aren't training inch by inch, one moment at a time, in overcoming our fear of pain, then we'll be very limited in how much we can help. We'll be limited in helping ourselves, and limited in helping anybody else. So, let's start with ourselves, just as we are, here and now.

# 5

# *Compassionate Abiding*

~~~>>>>>~

WHEN SOMETHING we find unpleasant occurs, our conditioning automatically clicks in and we have a strong
reaction. There is a practice we can do right
then to help us stay present and awake. It
is called compassionate abiding. Compassionate abiding provides a way to no longer
invest our reactions with so much absolute

truth. We can see our interpretations and our opinions as just that—our interpretations and opinions. We no longer have to be under their control, or have them color everything we think and do. Strong reactions will continue to arise, just the way the weather changes. But each of us can develop our ability to not escalate the emotions so that they become a nightmare and increase our suffering.

For the purpose of doing this practice, try to connect with a feeling of aversion to something. Whether this is a smell, a sound, or a memory of a person, an event, dark places, snakes—whatever it is, use your discursive mind to help you contact the feeling of aversion. And then, as much as possible, apply the technique of letting the thoughts go so that you can abide in the experience of aversion as a felt quality.

For some people it's just felt in the body. Sometimes it's more atmospheric. Imagine someone asking you, "What does aversion feel like?" You want to find out. Even if you can't put it into words, you want to have a nonverbal experience of dislike.

Once you've contacted that, if you can contact it, then breathe in; instead of pushing the feeling of aversion away, invite it in, but without believing in the judgments and opinions about it, just contacting the feeling free of your interpretation. You can do this for yourself as a way of approaching what you find repulsive, and you can also do it with the wish that all people, who just like you are hooked by the power of aversion, could not act it out, could not become its slave. In this way your own discomfort can connect you with the aversion and pain of other people and awaken your compassion.

So this exercise of compassionate abiding, and in this case specifically, abiding with the experience of aversion, consists of breathing in the negative feeling and then relaxing outward. Then you breathe the feeling in and relax outward again and again. You could do this for five minutes or for hours or anytime, on the spot, when aggressive feelings arise. We do this for ourselves and all other people who feel prejudice and disgust and have no way of working with it so it escalates into self-denigration, into jealousy, and violence, and creates endless suffering all over the world.

We contact the aversion, experiencing it as fully as possible as we breathe in, and then we relax as we breathe out. We let the feeling be a basis for compassion, and also—gradually, over time—we realize that it's like a phantom; when we stay with it in this way, the aversion dissolves; it's not an opponent that we're struggling against; it's not anything except energy that gets solidified and that we justify and then, on the basis of that justification, we hurt people.

There's a quote that is usually attributed to Carl Jung that says, "The only way out is through." This is very much the approach here. It's not a way of getting rid of strong emotions, nor is it a way of indulging in them. Gradually we learn to simply abide with our experience just as it is, without building it up or tearing it down, without getting carried away, knowing our own unfabricated energy as the same fluid, dynamic, unpindownable energy that courses through all living things.

# 6

# *Positive Insecurity*

I N THIS BOOK I've been exploring the topic of peace at the personal level, the level of each of us working with our own minds and our hearts. But I want to make it very clear that however we work with our minds and hearts these days will impact the future of this planet.

The Buddhist teachings on karma, put

very simply, tell us that each moment in time—whether in our personal lives or in our life together on earth—is the result of our previous actions. According to these teachings, what we experience in the present is the result of the seeds we've sown for hundreds of years, over the course of many lifetimes. It's also the case that the seeds you sowed yesterday have their result in your own life today. And the seeds that the United States has sown in the last year, five years, fifty years, hundred years, and so forth are having their impact on the world right now—and not just what the United States has sown but all the countries that are involved in the world situation today, being as painful as it is. We've been sowing these seeds for a long time.

I know many of us feel a kind of despair about whether all this can ever unwind itself. The message of this book is that it has to happen at the level of individuals working with their own minds, because even if these tumultuous times are the result of seeds that have been sown and reaped by whole nations, these nations of course are made up of millions of people who, just like ourselves, want happiness.

So whatever we do today, tomorrow, and every day of our lives until we die sows the seeds for our own future in this lifetime and sows the seeds for the future of this planet. The Buddhist teachings also say that the seeds of our present-day actions will bear fruit hundreds of years from now. This may seem like an impossibly long time to wait, but if you think in terms of sowing seeds for your children's future and for your grandchildren's future and your grandchildren's grandchildren's future, perhaps that's more real and immediate to you. Nevertheless how we work with ourselves today is how a shift away from widespread aggression will come about.

The other day I was given an article that contained a quote by the German political thinker Rudolph Bahro. He writes, "When an old culture is dying, the new culture is created by those people who are not afraid to be insecure."

I suppose some would question whether an old culture is dying right now, but somehow it rings true for me that we're in a time of major change, a major transition in the world, and many of us are rather nervous about where we're headed. But this quotation offers the intriguing suggestion that the new culture will be created by those who are not afraid to be insecure. The

writer and teacher Alan Watts titled one of
his books *The Wisdom of Insecurity*. Bahro's
quote is pointing us in that direction.

You can think of insecurity as a moment in time that we experience over and
over in our lives. When you feel insecurity,
whether you're feeling it in the middle
of the night out of nowhere or whether
it's constant, there is a groundless and unformed quality to it. As I've already said,
the Buddhist teachings suggest that this
kind of insecurity can serve as a direct path
to freedom—if you can stop yourself from
setting off the chain reaction of aggression
and misery.

You can think of the groundlessness and
openness of insecurity as a chance that
we're given over and over to choose a fresh
alternative. Things happen to us all the time

that open up the space. This spaciousness, this wide-open, unbiased, unprejudiced space is inexpressible and fundamentally good and sound. It's like the sky. Whenever you're in a hot spot or feeling uncomfortable, whenever you're caught up and don't know what to do, you can find someplace where you can go and look at the sky and experience some freshness, free of hope and fear, free of bias and prejudice, just completely open. And this is accessible to us all the time. Space permeates everything, every moment of our lives.

You could say that this spaciousness and simplicity, dwelling in that place ongoingly, would be a description of the enlightened or awakened state. But even for people like you and me, it's accessible all the time. We experience it very directly whenever we feel wonder, whenever we feel awe, and whenever there's a sudden shock. For example, you're walking across the street, and someone yells an obscenity at you. Before the chain reaction starts, before the aggression or the habitual pattern clicks in, there's a shock, an open space. There's just the fact that something has stunned you, someone has just insulted you, the ground has just fallen out from under your feet. Before trying to get back on solid ground by following the habitual chain reaction, you can pause and breathe deeply in and breathe deeply out. Never underestimate the power of this simple pause.

I do this as a practice whenever the rug gets pulled out, whenever the ground shifts, whether it's something hurting my feelings, or if suddenly, out of nowhere, something shocking happens that brings up panic. Whenever there's that sting of pain,

I practice pausing, because I know that that moment is precious. This is the instruction that I've been given, and it's the one I've offered in this book. If we pause and breathe in and out, then we can have the experience of timeless presence, of the inexpressible wisdom and goodness of our own minds. We can look out at the world with fresh eyes and hear things with fresh ears. In that pause—which is free of bias, free of thinking, just given to us on a silver platter by this person who insulted us—we can relax and open. The sting of that ordinary shock can lead us to a new way of living.

All of our aggressive speech, our aggressive actions, starts in the mind. It starts when we get triggered, when we get hooked. This is the moment of truth for those people who wish to stop watering the seeds of anger and prejudice. When our lives become uncomfortable, rather than automatically watering these seeds of aggression, we can burn them up.

I often wondered why it is that when I get hooked, when I'm resentful for example, and I breathe with it instead of acting out, it feels like I'm sitting in the middle of the fire. I asked Kongtrul Rinpoche about this. He said, "Because by not doing the habitual thing, you're burning up the seeds of aggression." As each individual works with it in this way, it's not just a minor thing. It's an opportunity we're given not only to connect with the inexpressible goodness of our minds and our hearts, but also to dissolve aggression in the world.

Someone once asked me, "What would it feel like to have burned up all those seeds, to be a person who no longer has any aggression?" The person who asked this was thinking that such a person might be pretty boring. No juice, no passion. I answered that I really wouldn't know from personal experience, but I imagine that such a person would be great company. If you dissolved your aggression, it would mean that other people wouldn't have to walk on eggshells around you, worried that something they might say would offend you. You'd be an accessible, genuine person. The awakened people that I've known are all very playful, curious, and unthreatened by things. They go into situations with their eyes and their hearts wide open. They have a real appetite for life instead of an appetite for aggression. They are, it seems, not afraid to be insecure.

In order to change our habits and burn

up the seeds of aggression, we have to develop an appetite for what I like to call positive groundlessness, or positive insecurity. Normally of course, we want to get away from that uncomfortable feeling. It just seems reasonable to want to do so. And it would be reasonable, except for the fact that you may have noticed that it doesn't really work. We've been trying the same ways of getting comfortable for as long as we can remember, and yet our aggression, our anxiety, our resentfulness don't seem to be getting any less. I'm saying that we need to develop an appetite for groundlessness; we need to get curious about it and be willing to pause and hang out for a while in that space of insecurity.

One of the methods I've touched on for doing this is when you notice that you're hooked, don't act out, don't repress, but let the experience pierce you to the heart. Another suggestion I've made is that when you notice that you're hooked, just pause and breathe deeply in and out, knowing that this is a moment in time that's impermanent, shifting, and changing. This insecurity that you're feeling is nothing monolithic. It's nothing solid. It's not graspable. It's passing. And you can breathe with it and relax with it, and let it pass through you.

Recently I was with Kongtrul Rinpoche and I asked him, "Rinpoche, you've been living in the West now for some time, and you know Western people well. What do you think is the most important advice that you could give to us?" He replied, "I think the most important thing that Westerners need to understand is guiltlessness." He went on to explain, "Even though we may make a lot of mistakes and we may mess up in all kinds of ways, all of that is impermanent, shifting, changing, and temporary. But fundamentally, our minds and hearts are not guilty. They are innocent."

So if at any moment of feeling guilty, insecure, and troubled you were to pause and let go of the words and start breathing slowly and deeply, you could let the whole drama unwind and unravel. If you could hang out in that uncomfortable yet impermanent, ineffable space, you might realize that all of this blaming of other people comes out of simply not being able to stay present.

If you want there to be peace—anything from peace of mind to peace on earth— here is the condensed instruction: stay with the initial tightening and don't spin off. Keep it simple.

---

And there's another essential ingredient: compassion. Train in keeping it simple in the vast context of all sentient beings. Point your finger randomly to any spot on the globe and you know for sure that there are beings there biting the hook. Almost everyone on the planet is addicted to spinning off, and the results aren't looking so good. If even a few of us practice keeping it simple—not making such a big deal out of pleasant and unpleasant—it will make a significant difference.

So the next time you feel yourself getting hooked, see if you can catch it. Can you feel yourself tightening? Can you feel yourself starting to erect protective barriers? Then pause and breathe with that unsettling energy. Somehow right there, in these moments that we're given over and over, we can realize that the insecurity that we're feeling has the potential of creating a new culture, one based on love and compassion rather than on fear and aggression. We can be part of creating a new culture for ourselves individually and for the world.

When you open yourself to the continually changing, impermanent, dynamic nature of your own being and of reality, you increase your capacity to love and care about other people and your capacity to not be afraid. You're able to keep your eyes open, your heart open, and your mind open. And you notice when you get caught up in prejudice, bias, and aggression. You develop an enthusiasm for no longer watering those negative seeds, from now until the day you die. And you begin to think of your life as offering endless opportunities to start to do things differently, endless opportunities to dissolve the seeds of war where they originate—in the hearts and minds of individuals like you and me.

# Resources

FOR INFORMATION about meditation instruction or to find a practice center near
you, please contact one of the following:

Shambhala International
1084 Tower Road
Halifax, Nova Scotia
Canada B3H 2Y5
phone: (902) 425-4275
fax: (902) 423-2750
website: www.shambhala.org

Shambhala Europe
Annostrasse 27-33
D50678 Köln, Germany
phone: 49-221-31024-10
fax: 49-221-31024-50
e-mail: europe@shambhala.org

Karmê Chöling
369 Patneaude Lane
Barnet, Vermont 05821
phone: (802) 633-2384
fax: (802) 633-3012
e-mail: karmecholing@shambhala.org

Shambhala Mountain Center
4921 Country Road 68C
Red Feather Lakes, Colorado 80545
phone: (970) 881-2184
fax: (970) 881-2909
e-mail: rmsc@shambhala.org

Gampo Abbey
Pleasant Bay, Nova Scotia
Canada BoE 2Po
phone: (902) 224-2752
e-mail: office@gampoabbey.org

Naropa University is the only accred-
ited, Buddhist-inspired university in North
America. For more information, contact:

Naropa University
2130 Arapahoe Avenue
Boulder, Colorado 80302
phone: (303) 444-0202
website: www.naropa.edu

Audio- and videotape recordings of
talks and seminars by Pema Chödrön are
available from:

Great Path Tapes and Books
330 East Van Hoesen Boulevard
Portage, Michigan 49002
phone: (269) 384-4167
fax: (425) 940-8456
e-mail: gptapes@aol.com
website: www.pemachodrontapes.org

Kalapa Recordings
1084 Tower Road
Halifax, Nova Scotia
Canada B3H 2Y5
phone: (902) 420-1118, ext. 19
fax: (902) 423-2750
e-mail: shop@shambhala.org
website: www.shambhalashop.com

Sounds True
735 Walnut Street
Boulder, Colorado 80302
phone: (800) 333-9185
website: www.soundstrue.com

# About the Author

PEMA CHÖDRÖN is an American Buddhist nun in the lineage of Chögyam Trungpa, the renowned Tibetan meditation master. She is resident teacher at Gampo Abbey, Cape Breton, Nova Scotia, the first Tibetan monastery in North America established for Westerners. She is the author of eight books including the best-selling *When Things Fall Apart* and *The Places That Scare You*.